MW01166267

# Guidebook for the Family with Alcohol Problems

**About the book:**

   The author explains the purposes of this book stating, "If you stand in close relationship with someone who is dependent upon alcohol and pills, this small book is for you — and for them. . . . Here I hope the both of you will find light on the illness and on the path of recovery. If someone you love needs treatment, you will need it too. . . . this book will take the mystery out of the process and aid your pilgrimage."

# Guidebook for the Family with Alcohol Problems

by James E. Burgin

First printing, June 1982

ISBN: 0-89486-155-7

Printed in the United States of America.

# CONTENTS

**Foreword**    vii

**Chapter One** — A Solution Becomes A Problem    1

**Chapter Two** — A Problem Becomes An Illness    9

**Chapter Three** — The Disease of the Family    15
    Emotional Response    17
    Behavioral Response    22
    Structural Response    24
    Crisis Response    27

**Chapter Four** — Treatment    29
    When the Chemically Dependent Person Seeks
        Treatment    30
    The Parallel Track of Early Recovery    35

**Chapter Five** — Recovery    43
    Reversal of Isolation    48
    Help for the Marriage    49
    The Children    56
    Relapse    57
    Spiritual Recovery    59

**Afterword** — Getting Help    61

Drink to me only with thine eyes,
  And I will pledge with mine;
Or leave a kiss but in the cup,
  And I'll not look for wine.

Ben Jonson, *To Celia*, 1616

# FOREWORD

I once heard a famous theologian in the process of confessing his own limited knowledge, say that everything he knew for sure could be written on a three by five inch card, in fairly large letters.

These few pages attempt to distill most of what I know as a result of having spent the years since 1970 in almost daily engagement with individuals, and families, struggling with alcoholism and other drug dependencies. Having written it, I am left with two impressions: how little room it takes up, and how much mystery remains.

The process of clarifying the mystery is what this book is about. How shall those of us who care deeply for persons suffering addiction understand their pain — and our own? And, understanding it, how shall we participate in healing — for them, for us, and for our relationship with them?

If you stand in close relationship with someone who is dependent upon alcohol and pills, this small book is for you — and for them. My hope is that you could discuss the book with them — thereby breaking the conspiracy of silence by which our culture allows these illnesses to progress unchecked.

Here I hope the both of you will find light on the illness and on the path of recovery. If someone you love needs treatment, you will need it too. My hope is that this book will help to take some of the mystery and fear out of that word "treatment" — and allow you both to step in. If you already have, I hope this book will illuminate the process and aid your pilgrimage.

What is written here, I have learned from patients, peers, a good psychotherapist and the two families I am a part of — it is all experiential learning.

Some of my teachers:

> My father who, because of his alcoholism, I never saw. Very few knew about alcoholism in 1937. The power of his absence and the silence of our family about it, taught me that alcoholism, like marriage, really is "till death do us part"; even when there is divorce.

> Joseph D. Chelette and George Dominick, ministers and mentors (one in his energy and one in his quietness) who gave me my first job in the addiction field, taught me how to think about addiction, and a way to engage the addicted individual emotionally.

> William B. Johnson, sometime colleague and all-time good friend. Bill and I worked together so closely for years that much of what is written here was created between us out of the miracle of dialogue.

> The three women in my life: mother — Ruth, wife — Eleanor, daughter — Ann, all of them helping me learn the difference between caring for and taking care of.

Appreciating that difference is where healing begins for those of us who love someone who hurts. Life being what it is, that includes us all. If you are still learning about this, as I am, I hope this small book helps.

James E. Burgin, M.Div.
Charleston, South Carolina
1982

# CHAPTER ONE
## A Solution Becomes a Problem

"No illness so profoundly affects the whole family as this one," said the counselor. Janet was surprised. This professional was referring to her husband's drinking problem as an illness. She felt relieved to have finally found someone who understood the stress she had been under, but she felt apprehensive, too.

Certainly something had been wrong with Dave, her husband. For the last year or so, the whole family had been puzzled and troubled by the unexplainable changes in his drinking. But an "illnesss"? Janet suddenly felt a little panicky. Dave wasn't that bad, was he?

In the uneasy silence, Janet's thoughts returned to the changes she had noticed in Dave, in their marriage, in herself, and yes, certainly in his drinking.

Although in the early years of their marriage Dave's drinking was "like anyone else's," Janet had noticed that during the last few years his drinking had become more and more important to him. It seemed to her that he drank too much, too often.

She had said nothing for a while and told herself that she didn't want to be a moralist about alcohol as her mother had been. Janet hoped perhaps the Florida vacation really would allow Dave to unwind, and then things would change.

When they didn't change, she began trying to discuss it and found Dave strangely defensive. He wouldn't talk about it. That was not like Dave. He often tended to be a private and sensitive man, but he was usually willing to talk about anything that was important between them.

Over the next several months their relationship seriously deteriorated as Dave was less and less responsive to the family. And Janet became more and more insistent that he do something to cut down on his drinking.

Dave was secretly scared. Alcohol had always been a pleasant part of his life, always bringing its predictable magic. It had been a part of their courtship, and champagne was served at their wedding! They still had the glass they had drunk from. Now the pleasure was not so dependable. The magic seemed to have disappeared. Were the days of wine and roses really gone? He could not believe so! How he tried to get them back. Maybe, if Janet would just drink with him. She used to, but had recently stopped. The more he thought about it, the more he felt her non-drinking a reproach.

In the magic time of the past, alcohol had helped him relax, feel less self-conscious, feel more at ease with people. It had been a real, workable solution for his shyness. Everyone said what fun he was at a party.

But something had changed. After the party last week, people had made it clear that he had been a pain. Yet, strangely, Dave could not remember much of it the next morning. Now he was really scared. Had the solution become a problem? He would cut down. Yes, for sure, he would try to control his drinking from now on.

As he tried, however, Janet noticed that he was even harder

to live with. He would become irritable, irrationally angry, and so nervous that he could not sit still. She witnessed his increasing nervousness, his attempts to calm it with more alcohol and then his attempts to calm it with tranquilizers from their family doctor. This doctor had been practically a friend of the family for many years. They couldn't tell him about the drinking.

Why was Dave so nervous? She feared the worst. Was he going crazy? She dared not share with anyone the fearful thought that she might be responsible. Dave frequently accused her in ways that made her wonder if he was right. Maybe if she quit pressuring him, he could regain his balance alone.

But Janet couldn't quit. Much as she told herself to give him room to work it out, she found her anxiety increasing. She continued to pressure him. She could no more quit than he could.

So, she was here talking with an alcoholism counselor. She was afraid he would use that word — "alcoholism"! But, he did seem able to help her think straight.

After the hour together, she remembered he had said, "Alcohol is a drug. Alcoholism is addiction to that drug. It *is* an illness. We don't know why it happens to one person in nine who drink."

That night of her first reaching out for professional help Janet and Dave sat watching television. A man was singing. They heard the words of the song as they never had before.

> The days of wine and roses
> Laugh and run away, like a child at play,
> Through the meadowland, toward a closing door,
> A door marked "Nevermore"
> That wasn't there before.
>
> The lonely night discloses
> Just a passing breeze,

> Filled with memories,
> Of the golden smile that introduced me to
> The days of wine and roses and you.*

"What did you do today?" asked Dave, attempting to break the spell the song cast over the room. "I went to see an alcoholism counselor," Janet replied, shocked at her own courage. For the rest of an uneasy evening the subject was dropped. The children sensed that a vague, but very real, cool uneasiness came over the house. They walked more carefully and quietly though they didn't know why. For the adults in the silence there was the unspoken understanding that a barrier had been crossed and that never again could they go back and pretend that it had not.

As she took her fear to bed, Janet felt also that somehow she was standing on firmer ground. "It's far from hopeless," the counselor had said. "As we look over what's been happening, it sounds like whatever problems you have in the marriage, the drinking itself has become a main problem. So, let's begin with the drinking and your confused, hurt and angry response to it. Really, as chronic diseases go, this one, addiction, is the most hopeful one for treatment. The prospect for recovery, particularly with early intervention, is quite good."

Dave and Janet's situation is typical. Because our culture is confused about what drinking means, it is very hard to decide objectively when alcohol is becoming a problem for someone, especially someone we live with or are close to. Drinking is often considered a sign of manliness, a sign of weakness, classy, crass, a sign of success, a sign of sinfulness. The drunk person we laugh at on Saturday night at the party and shake our heads about the next morning is the same person.

The subject of alcohol is such an emotionally charged issue in our history and in our present feelings, that everyone becomes an armchair expert. You don't have to listen to much conversation before someone is willing to tell you exactly how he or she feels about alcohol and other mood-altering drugs — "as long as a person avoids the 'hard stuff' and just drinks beer or wine it will be O.K. . . . ; as long as you don't drink in the morning . . . ; if you just don't drink alone . . . ; well, he never misses a day's work, so . . . ; surely not her, she's such a fine person . . . ; he doesn't drink every day. Why just this winter he went a month and touched nothing, so . . ." How is Janet to think clearly amid all this confusion? And yet, it is just to such folk wisdom that we often find ourselves turning for answers.

When we are looking for an understanding of the causes of chemical dependency, we must reach back into our *culture* and the attitudes and values we collectively hold. The use of mood-changing substances in our culture is rising. We pretend that alcoholism and drug dependence are grossly "abnormal" conditions that exist in a "normal" culture, and we cannot understand how such extreme deviance could arise. The fact is, that in twentieth century America these illnesses arise out of a culture that wants to be anesthetized; a culture that has lost the old values and not yet found new ones; a culture that has no shared consensus as to what is the normal social use of alcohol; a culture that wants to believe that there are easy solutions outside ourselves to the internal problem of being human. The commercials for alcoholic beverages and medications on television vividly illustrate socially acceptable escape.

Ours is a culture where use moves into abuse unnoticed. When one becomes intoxicated and explains it by saying, "I really needed a drink tonight . . . boy what a day!" — that is drug abuse. It is not social drinking. It is drug abuse because it represents self-medication of stress by use of the drug, alcohol. It is our most socially approved drug, but a drug nevertheless, and it doesn't require a prescription. Custom, ritual, and tradition dictate that for many of us, part of adult recreation will include the use of a powerful mind-altering drug — alcohol. Furthermore, large numbers of us believe that "heavy drinking" is normal and would be quite offended at the suggestion that it represents "drug abuse."

This is not intended to reflect an anti-alcohol sentiment. It may well be, if it were possible to calculate such things, that alcohol has been more of a blessing than a curse. In any event, the reality is that it is important to us, along with a host of other mood-altering chemicals (from caffeine to nicotine to tranquilizers) and is here to stay.

Understanding our culture may help us to be less surprised that there is such prevalence of these problems and perhaps give us more understanding of those who contract the illness. We grow up with the suggestion, reinforced daily by all of our communication and entertainment media, that drinking is sophisticated, sexy, manly, a badge of the modern self-actualized woman, smart, a sign of affluence, a good social lubricant, a preferred way to relax, and a problem solver. It is not too difficult to understand that some of us who strive for all of these things will become dependent upon the substance.

When searching for causes, we must examine the possibility of an *inheritance* factor. Research studies of adopted children suggest this possibility. These studies demonstrate a significantly greater incidence of addictive illness among adopted children who had at least one natural parent who was addicted.

This certainly does not suggest that children of alcoholic parents will of necessity develop alcoholism. It may suggest, however, that they have a somewhat greater risk of developing the illness. If a parent or grandparent is an alcoholic, we may be wise to limit our own drinking.

Research is also investigating the possibility of *biochemical* factors in these diseases. It may be that the body chemistry of some of us handle addictive drugs in a different way. This may be a possible explanation of the fact that oriental people have an adverse physical reaction to alcohol. Alcohol may come to mean more to some of us than to others because it can create a greater subjective sense of pleasure for some.

As a result of these factors, and perhaps some factors yet undiscovered, some of us become trapped in an escalating cycle of substance use. This occurs so slowly and insidiously that it is hardly noticed. More and more pleasures come to be associated with having a drink. Feelings of tension more predictably serve as a cue for the remedy that works quickest. Remorse for the mistakes while last under the influence becomes the reason for the next occasion of abuse. It is as though one is living in an ever narrowing circle with alcohol at the center.

This is a process too diverse to illustrate through the lives of one couple. Rather, we will follow the usual themes, issues, potential pitfalls and opportunities, and illustrate them through the lives of a host of fellow sufferers who have come this way before.

Hopefully, if you or someone you love needs to walk this road, this book may serve as a guide. In this instance, the guide only knows the road. In ways particular to you alone, you will fill in the special characteristics of that road: the rough places and smooth, the weariness and the hope, the weather along the way.

To have some idea of the journey in advance can be helpful. But we have no need to anticipate all the particulars. It is enough that we walk — one day at a time.

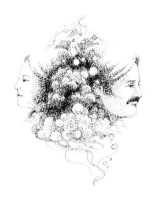

# CHAPTER TWO
## A Problem Becomes an Illness

Substance dependency progresses so slowly that the person developing it does not perceive when he or she crosses the line from social use to abusive use or from abusive use to addictive use.

What Janet and Dave would have opportunity to learn, along with millions of others, is that while the popular "wisdom" about drinking is often more confusing than helpful, there are specific indicators that one's drinking has become a progression that has led to the illness of substance dependency. Such indicators are:

**Frequent Overdose:** Most of us would become very concerned if we learned that our neighbor's daughter had overdosed on drugs. Being drunk is simply being overdosed on the drug alcohol. The average 150 pound person can handle about an ounce and a half of liquor (or one twelve-ounce can of beer, or three ounces of wine) an hour.

The thing to remember is that most people don't get drunk

every time they drink. The person for whom most drinking occasions lead to being drunk may be headed for trouble.

**Increased Tolerance:** This refers to the body's ability to adapt so as to take in larger doses of a drug (including alcohol) to get the same or similar effect that a smaller dose used to produce.

Whereas two drinks in an hour used to get a person woozy, now that same amount has hardly any effect at all — it takes four to feel anything. This bodily adaptation to the drug is what we are witnessing when we ask, "How can anyone possibly drink that much?"

**Loss of Control:** This symptom means that on any given drinking occasion an individual cannot be sure of being able to stop before overdose. At times he or she may be able to control the drinking through unusual effort, but it is an uncertain occurrence. Experience shows that the brief instances of control often become a "tapering on" over several days or weeks.

That control is an issue at all may be a danger signal. The drinking person who is not in trouble does not usually worry about control or boast about the ability to control. We try to control that which causes us problems. What happens, for people getting in trouble, is that with an ever increasing certainty, they lose control. Though they promise themselves and others to stop at a certain level, they simply cannot count on being able to do this. The attempts to regain the lost control are legion; switching to another substance — "Maybe if I just drank beer"; switching the place — "Maybe if I only drank at home"; switching the time — "Maybe if I only drank on weekends."

**Withdrawal:** What happens when a person stops drinking

after a rather heavy period? Most people who drink are familiar with the "hangover." Withdrawal goes beyond this discomfort and may include irritability, nervousness, high susceptability to stimulation (as a noise that easily startles), sleep disturbance, elevated blood pressure, and/or shakiness (either inside, or in one's hands) that more alcohol will calm.

We generally assume there are only two states a person may be in with regard to alcohol; drunk or sober. For the person in trouble with drinking, there is a third state that can occupy more time than either of these two — withdrawal. It can last, at least in its milder aspects, for weeks after the drinking has stopped. This is why the alcoholic is "harder to live with" when he stops drinking and becomes what his family assumes is "sober." The symptoms of withdrawal lead many to conclude that they, or a family member, are experiencing a nervous problem or mental breakdown. The reality is that the great majority of these persons will discover that their "nerves" are no longer a problem once they go three weeks without any alcohol or other mood-altering substances.

The acute phase of withdrawal usually passes, with good medical care, in five to ten days. Chronic withdrawal (or sub-acute withdrawal), however, may last for weeks after drinking is stopped and includes continuing sleep disturbance, foggy thinking, depression, and irritability.

**Blackouts:** These appear to be temporary amnesia; forgetting what was done or said while under the influence of a drug.

Since some of what is forgotten can include things that have hurt and angered others, family members sometimes feel this symptom is not real — "Oh, he's just lying to cover his embarrassment." On the contrary, blackouts as usually experienced by their victims are very frightening. Early in my experience one man convinced me they were real as he pleaded, "I hid two thousand dollars somewhere yesterday, and I can't remember where. What's happening to me? Am I going crazy?"

It is important to distinguish this from lying or going crazy. It is caused by the effect of alcohol on the brain.

**Loss of Drug Effectiveness:** The drug simply quits doing for its user what he wants it to do. "It's like when I start drinking, I feel I'm going to get the old feeling back . . . and it does last for fifteen maybe thirty minutes . . . but then it's like I lose it and just begin getting depressed instead."

Understanding these several symptoms can help us cut through the many myths about defining alcoholic drinking. Most of those mythical definitions are designed to ease our anxiety about our own drinking or that of a loved one. By this clever footwork, an alcoholic is simply whatever I'm not. "If I still have my job and family, isn't it obvious that an alcoholic is the one on skid row, or one who has lost those things I still have?"

These social definitions simply do not hold up. For example, it can be clearly shown that the skid row alcoholic represents less than five percent of the alcoholic population of over ten million in the United States. Most alcoholics still have jobs, homes, and families. They live on your street and on mine.

Alcoholism is not a matter of *how much* we drink. It is not a matter of *when* we drink, or *how often*. It is not a matter of *where* we drink. It is a matter of *what happens when we drink*: frequent overdose, increased tolerance, loss of control, withdrawal, blackouts, and loss of drug effectiveness. The reaching for mythical social definitions of it may be an indication of one further, and very dangerous, symptom.

**Denial:** If a couple can think back to the earliest time when one of them began to express concern about the other's drinking, the response was probably something like, "Don't be silly . . . I can handle it . . . and stop any time I want to!" The thing that makes this so dangerous is that while it may be used by the troubled drinker to hold down a lot of fear and anxiety, at least partially and temporarily, he or she really *believes* it. This symptom is called *denial*. It represents the heart of the emotional adaptation to alcoholism.

It is important that we distinguish denial from lying. Lying is what I do to fool someone else when I am caught with my hand in the cookie jar. Denial is what I do to fool myself when I need to believe that just a few more cookies won't make me put on any weight. That way I can eat the cookies and not feel anxious. This process works so effectively that I don't even have to "think about it."

Another component of the denial process is the projection of the blame onto another person or persons. "Well, if you hadn't baked the cookies so late in the afternoon that the whole house was filled with the tempting aroma when I came home, I wouldn't have eaten them." Or to illustrate it in terms of the family troubled by drinking: "He drinks because she scolds, he thinks." (Ogden Nash). "If my wife/husband were not (choose one) domineering, withdrawn, independent, dependent, gone all the time, always under foot, angry, passive, giving me such a hard time about drinking, I could control it."

The world of the person who is becoming addicted is full of fear and terrible guilt feelings. What we are looking at here is a defense against all of that. A defense in which some of the intolerable guilt is projected onto another, and thereby temporarily relieved.

One reason projection of blame works so well, and is so frequently accepted and believed by those who live with someone struggling with their drinking, is that we have all been raised in a psychologically-minded age. We have been taught to look for the "real," by which we usually mean the secret, underlying reason why we behave in certain ways. This insight has helped us much in efforts to understand ourselves. It has limited usefulness, however, in attempts to understand alcoholism.

This is a complex illness. When all the research is in, it may very well show a large involvement of body chemistry in the cause of alcoholism. The best we know now is that the disease seems to be related to physical, mental, emotional, spiritual and social dimensions of life. Certainly the illness is too complex to explain it by saying that "the reason" a woman drinks herself into destruction of large elements of herself is because her husband relates the way he does.

The folly of such a shallow approach has been demonstrated untold times by many couples who have sincerely "tried marriage counseling." After months of therapy many know all the "reasons" one of them drinks destructively, but the drinking continues. Personal growth and/or growth of a marriage, will not alone serve to arrest addiction, though they will certainly be an important element in complete recovery once the use of chemicals has been arrested.

# CHAPTER THREE
## The Disease of the Family

Being in close emotional relationship to an alcoholic or other substance dependent person produces in most of us a pattern of interaction that over time becomes a syndrome as real as the addiction itself. That syndrome has been labeled by various students as "co-dependency," "co-alcoholism," "near-alcoholism," or "enabling." These terms define a group of behaviors designed to protect the alcoholic. Their real effect is to enable the disease to proceed untreated because the substance dependent person does not have the opportunity to experience the direct consequences of the drug use. It is important to see this response as a "dis-ease" in its own right. After this interaction pattern has been going on for a sufficient length of time, it achieves a life of its own.

Deep down in the nature of a commitment to intimacy is the feeling that we have a moral obligation to care for those we love. We feel that we should protect them if we can, aid their pilgrimage and support their growth. We would even heal them if we could. Like so many of the deep emotional realities of life, these feelings have potential for both good and evil. They create and enrich relationships.

The destructive potential exists because no one, not even one who is sick, wants to be "kept" by another. One of the great Eastern religions tells the tale of the master-teacher putting to his pupil the question, "Why are you angry at me? I have not tried to help you." A close relationship in which one party attempts to take care of the other moves of necessity toward dependency, anger, resentment, and, finally, destruction.

Any of us who could, would avoid such a course for an important relationship. And yet, if left unchecked, the natural drift of our relationships with chemically dependent people is precisely in this direction. The drift into this syndrome is accompanied by a lot of fear. But drift detected is more subject to correction. Drifting down a river where there are familiar sights is a vastly different thing than being adrift in the ocean. A look at the signposts along the way may serve, along with someone to talk with, to reduce the fear and raise some options.

It seems useful to view the development of the syndrome as a progression of an *emotional response* to a *behavioral response* to a *structural response* to a *crisis response.* Each is a response to the drug dependent person, but also a response to who *we* are deep down inside. Because this is so and because family relationships change under the influence of addictive illness, thorough treatment must pay as much attention to the pattern of this response as to the addiction itself. The interaction patterns and the changes in family relationships do not necessarily heal with the cessation of the substance use.

For these reasons most addiction counselors will, early in the relationship, come up with some version of the suggestion: "Well, I believe I'm beginning to understand how destructive her drinking (or his use of the pills) has been; now let's talk about your reaction to all this — how have you tried to cope?"

## Emotional Response

As *fear* increases that a loved one, or valued friend or co-worker is getting into trouble with his or her drinking or pill-taking, we frequently experience a *denial* that parallels their own. Remember that denial is different from lying. It is an unconscious defense mechanism used without conscious thought to control fear and anxiety. It sounds like this, "Well, yes, he overdid it a bit last night, but it's not that bad. He could stop if he really wanted to. Why just last year he went a couple of months with nothing." Or, "She an alcoholic? Don't be silly. Anyone who drinks too much will have a bad hangover and be a little shaky. She never neglects the kids." Or, "Maybe, if I just cover for him this time it won't happen again." Or, "Yes, he had to be hospitalized for nerves and chest pains last month, but he'll be all right. He's even cut down on his drinking." Or even, "She an addict? Come on! The doctor prescribed those pills for her." And finally, "Well, yes, he drank too much . . . but he was such a fine man. I can't believe his wife. Imagine calling him an alcoholic!"

Denial is emotional blindness used to control anxiety. Its use is reinforced by the stereotypical attitudes in our culture about these illnesses. Who wouldn't deny the existence of a problem that could lead to severe social judgment and ostracism. This is slowly changing, but the reality of today is that dependent persons are still too often judged as morally weak.

Denial leads to well-meant, but destructive, attempts to explain to the children: "It's nothing . . . Mom is just upset again . . . just be still . . . don't irritate her and she'll be better in the morning." The use of denial in this way makes it difficult for children to know what is real. It is essential to the process of emotional and intellectual maturing that we learn to distinguish what is real and what is not.

Bailing the other person out, covering his or her tracks,

neutralizing the consequences of drug-related behavior — these attempts to rescue the dependent member express denial. The family really wants to believe it is up against a situation, not an illness. You can rescue another person from a situation — do something to make it better, mop up the spilt milk, give or loan them something to "tide them over," but you cannot rescue a person from a severe, life-threatening, chronic illness. For that, there is only treatment to teach the person to live with the illness.

As an example: A fine pastor-therapist saw a new patient one afternoon. After an hour and a half together in which the man opened up to the therapist about his fear of what was happening as a result of his drinking, patient and therapist agreed upon a diagnosis of alcoholism and a course of treatment. The man signed a form requesting that the therapist write his employer a letter indicating the diagnosis, treatment plan, and recommending time off from work to get treatment. The therapist wrote the letter which the man took with him to present to his employer the next day. At precisely nine o'clock the next morning, the therapist's phone rang. It was the man's wife, "We've decided that my husband isn't alcoholic . . . he's going back to work . . . we can work this thing out." "Just a moment," the therapist said. And he went to retrieve the man's chart. Coming back to the phone he continued: "This is the Mr. Y who came to see me just yesterday?"

"Yes."

"This is the Mr. Y who described to me the rapid increase in his drinking over the last two years, the blackouts, the inability to control the amount he drinks, the terrible inability to sleep, shakiness the next morning after heavy drinking, the arguments with you over drinking and several attempts to stop which have been unsuccessful over about the last year?"

"Yes, but he isn't alcoholic. I'm going to call his boss and explain his absence for the last few days. I'll help him stop drinking, and we'll be all right."

This woman was not stupid, nor was she deliberately destructive. She was scared. Her attempts to rescue, her denial of the severity of the illness, her defining it as a situation to be remedied rather than an illness to be treated would delay the possibility of successful intervention.

The emotional response to addictive illness in a family member frequently has its roots in guilt feelings. Our culture, and much of our humor, often implies that if someone drinks too much it's someone else's fault. "Did you hear the joke about the man who came home drunk and his wife said . . ." The assumption behind many of these stories is that what his wife says causes him to continue drinking.

Guilt of this proportion cannot be long sustained or tolerated. Often, in substance dependent families the guilt is projected. Ogden Nash has described this so well in his poem:

> "He drinks because she scolds, he thinks,
> She thinks she scolds because he drinks,
> And neither will admit what's true
> That he's a sot and she's a shrew."

Poetry through its potent, distilled essence of human experience plunges us quickly into the heart of things. These lines illuminate the projective blaming between alcoholic and spouse in reaction to their guilt feelings. (This projection sustains the illusion that one person is to blame.) The projection prevents each of the partners from developing a self-awareness which might permit consideration of change. Each is trapped in his or her own dilemma — the substance dependent person in dependency; the spouse in the equally familiar and repetitive patterns of behavior.

The children in addicted families also experience this

projection of responsibility. Subtly or directly, they too often get the message, "Mind your father tonight. You know he drinks when he gets upset!" The use of projective blaming makes it difficult to know what is real. The child who is a born mediator or peacemaker is trapped because his or her resources are often inadequate to the task of helping the family. Because of this kind of projection, many of us grow up feeling that if someone we love is in trouble, it is because we have not adequately done our job. It is essential to the process of maturing that we learn to distinguish what we are responsible for and what we are not responsible for.

*Grief* also often characterizes the emotional response of the family to addiction. The family has lost a part of their old life with a significant member. Not a clean, clear, loss that can be confirmed by death and the rituals that lead to mourning and healing, but a chronic extended period of loss with no visible end. There is a physical presence, but significant response, sexual function, and support are often lost.

This grief reaction of the family can be hidden. The substance-abusing behavior is so remarkable that the quiet response of the "good child" who mourns for his former experience with a healthy parent is overlooked. The spouse who grieves for the loss of passion is forgotten.

The old song, "There is a Tavern in the Town" — a good old ribald drinking song, right? Words for a celebration, right? Wrong! If you have ever heard it sung as the blues song that it really is, you may never forget it. Its words belong to the *spouse*, not to the drinking person. They tell the pain of loss and the grief of parting.

> "There is a tavern in the town
> And there my true love sits him down
> And drinks his wine 'mid laughter free,
> And never, never, thinks of me.

"Adieu, Adieu, Adieu, kind friends, adieu,
I can no longer stay with you,
I'll hang my harp on a weeping willow tree,
And may the world go well with thee."

A wife said to me, so full of pain she was giddy and a little
silly in trying to control it, "It's like I've lost him to a bottle . . . if
it had been another woman, I could fight back . . . but a bottle
. . . Ha!" Who can she fight? And as we talked, it was soon
apparent that just like someone who has lost a relative in death,
part of her "fight" was directed at herself. "Maybe if I had loved
him enough . . . was woman enough."

So, just as one who is bereaved, she needed someone to
listen as she poured out her grief. Someone to help her
understand that the spouse is also a victim of the disease.
Someone to help her separate feelings toward the lost one from
feelings toward herself, so that she could eventually get past this
grief.

When we are abandoned and in a time of grief, we usually
experience some anger along with the more obvious sadness.
The movement and direction that anger takes is important. It
can be directed toward ourselves as the woman in the example
above was doing. It can be directed toward the one who
abandoned us, "How could she do this to me again?" Or, it can
simply be held in and not given any direction. When this
happens, we usually talk about our "frustration" or
"resentment" or "hurt," rather than calling it anger.

One man, a gentle soul who had found it impossible to "be
mad at someone who is sick," had instead for some time been
doing many of the household tasks of his alcoholic wife. His
anger was obvious to everyone but himself. Because he was
afraid to hurt his wife, he was the one who was hurting as his
resentment ate away at his energy.

In a counseling session, he found it possible one day to take the suggestion that since his sick wife was not present to be hurt he might give his feeling of resentment a voice and let it speak for itself. Haltingly at first and then with a rush of feeling, he found himself with clenched fists, beating on the arm of his chair saying, "She has no idea what I've been through. I know she's sick, but I can't help it. I don't want to hate her, but I've got some needs too!" Indeed, he did. How important it was to begin to share the anger that resulted when the alcoholic spouse was no longer able to adequately meet this man's needs.

## Behavioral Response

The collision of the emotions described in the previous section leads to a set of behavioral responses to the addiction and to one's inner self. Reality intrudes. The denial eventually breaks down for family and friends. It is as though one day, as the illness progresses and worsens, the people who are significant to the substance dependent person decide that since it can no longer be denied, they must do something about it.

At this point, unless they obtain the help of Al-Anon or professional care, the family is at risk for developing a series of patterned behaviors that may be designated a *chronic, progressive, disease response pattern*. A chronic progressive disease response pattern has remarkable similarity whatever the chronic disease involved, heart disease, tuberculosis, cancer, diabetes, epilepsy, asthma and severe allergies, or addiction.

Joe comes home from four weeks in the hospital with a heart attack. His doctor has said, "Joe, you're going to have to take it easy, but don't make an invalid out of yourself. You can even take some moderate exercise. We'll talk about it." But when Joe gets home, his family are dealing not only with him, but with their own anxieties. So they sit him in the easy chair, bring him everything he needs, constantly remind him not to stress himself. They, as we say, "love him to death." They are caught in their chronic progressive disease response pattern.

This seems to have its foundation in the loss of control of the addicted person over the amount and frequency of intake. This reality, and the feelings of the spouse about it, leads most spouses of addicted persons into some *attempt to take control* of what appears as a deteriorating situation.

The strategies are many. In this effort to control, spouses are frequently prepared to try to outwit, shame, accuse, beg, threaten, outfox, in short, willing to try anything that seems to hold some hope of reinstituting control.

And it doesn't work. This pattern is a losing battle. If the family pours out the booze, the addict does not forget where the liquor store is. If the family extracts promises, the chemically dependent person gives them, then breaks them, and then feels remorse. The addicted family member experiences the controlling power of this cycle of crisis and repentance and pays a price of guilt. The spouse experiences more and more the feeling of loss of the very control the promises were designed to assert. The effort to control is literally a "no win situation" for everyone.

When any of us stay in a "no win situation" too long, invest too much energy in it, we come to feel, quite accurately, that we are "banging our head up against a stone wall." We feel stuck and powerless. And those feelings are the source of anger and depression. Anger and depression may represent extremes in the emotional life of the spouse of the addicted individual. One day the feeling is, "So help me if she drinks or takes those pills again, I'll kill her." And the next day, "What's the matter with me? Maybe if I tried harder to understand, didn't press her so about it, she would be all right. Maybe it's my fault."

In this manner, an ever widening behavioral reaction involving the addicted member of the family is perpetuated. The essence of this behavioral pattern is an effort to control his or her behavior. The result of that response is an increasing sense of frustration and panic growing from the awareness that, despite increased efforts, things are more and more out of control.

## Structural Response

Things having progressed this far, the whole family has now reorganized its structure to accommodate the reality of having a dysfunctional member. Families are systems of human relationships that are in constant, vital, shifting imbalance. Any change in one member affects the entire family.

Shortly after he had published his classic book on mental health and illness called *The Vital Balance*, Dr. Karl Menninger said that he wished it had been titled *The Vital Imbalance*. What keeps life (and families) healthy and moving forward is our capacity to allow, experience, tolerate, and adjust to constant imbalances. Children never learn to walk as long as they maintain perfect balance. We have to become imbalanced by standing on one foot while placing the other forward if we are to create a new balance.

Families are similar. Members grow through learning how to change relationships and be changed by them. When this process fails, to whatever degree, our families produce people who are rigid, inflexible, and at risk for undue stress in this changing, unpredictable world.

Chronic disease represents a deviation from the normal pattern of constantly shifting change that characterizes vital imbalances. Its symptoms are rather constant and predictable from one day to the next. This stands in marked contrast to the life of the emotionally and physically whole person. His or her life has more range, more diversity, and more change than the life of one chronically ill.

The same is true of families. Families struggling to adapt to a chemically ill member get locked into rigid inflexible balances that probably will not serve the needs of all members very well.

The family reorganizes to accommodate an addictive illness that may no longer be entirely denied. Since control is lost, the family reorganizes around the expectation that one member will be out-of-control and floundering.

This structural adaptation to addiction, reorganizing the family to accommodate it, brings a certain level of resolution. (It seems to solve some problems.) But it is done at great expense.

For example, a wife and mother who always stays close to home to watch out for, and protect a family from, a chemically dependent husband and father accomplishes something. But at what expense to herself? And at what expense to the marital relationship? Self-restriction for the sake of someone else leads almost invariably to feelings of hatred for that other person. Investing too much in the care of another leads almost invariably to social isolation for the caretaker. It is as though the closer we get to the sick family member the less we are able to see other facets of our own lives and nurture other relationships.

Or, another example: when a husband and father, denied the sexual responsiveness of a wife who is overdosed on mood-changing chemicals, reorganizes the family system by seeking an outside partner, he accomplishes something. But at what expense to himself? What will it cost him to try to be number one to two women?

The reorganization that takes place during this stage of the addictive illness occurs because the illness becomes the all-consuming focus of family life and attention. One of the side effects of this is child neglect. The energy that used to go to child rearing now has to be assigned to the more basic task of stabilizing chaos. Some studies have shown that while there is some increase in child abuse in addicted families, the greater problem is child neglect.

Children, great adapters that they are, find ways to accommodate to this change in family structure. The child with one parent who is chronically dysfunctional learns to not count on that parent. More and more the child goes to the other parent and excludes the addicted one. Or it can work in just the opposite way. The child perceives the non-addicted spouse as "the one who is always hollering" and gravitates more exclusively toward the addicted parent. In either case, the heart of the distress is quite similar. The unity of the parenting pair is broken, and while the child may experience the resulting increase in independence and power for himself as pleasurable, he also experiences fear.

More than not counting on one of the parents, children in this situation may learn not to count on that part of themselves that identifies with that parent. "If mother is like this, I won't be like mother." "If father acts like that, he sure is different from me." Here can be laid the foundation for a long and painful struggle with identity— the place where we balance those qualities in all of us that are soft, caring, nurturing; and those qualities that are strong, assertive, and structuring.

Children frequently go to the behavioral extremes of compliance or deviance as they participate in the structural changes in the family. Perceiving that something is very wrong in the family, it is as though they decide to either shape up to remedy the situation, or to act up in such a way that their parents will be forced (as the child imagines it) to shape up and discipline them.

A twenty-eight-year-old woman came for therapy. She had been raised in a home where, during her childhood, the family was struggling with addictive illness. As a result of her attempts to help her parents, she decided that she wanted to be a professional helper. She prepared herself and was a very effective member of her profession. But it took too much out of her. She felt too responsible for her patients and dealing with her resulting depression kept her from giving them the care they needed. It was not surprising when she said one day, "It's crazy . . . but I just feel like I want to play with dolls." On further reflection it did not seem crazy. In fact, it made a great deal of sense. Early in her life, when she should have been responding as a child by playing with dolls, she had felt the need to act like an adult and take care of her parents. Now, belatedly, her time had come. She could let herself experience her wish to play with dolls.

## Crisis Response

If the structural adaptation does not lead to a total reorganization of the family through divorce, the family will move toward some sort of crisis that makes it clear to at least one member that things have got to change—now! At that point they reach for help.

This *crisis* is a very different thing from the repetitive hassles that characterize families struggling with addiction. A patient made the difference very clear. "Why are you here for help at this particular time?" the counselor asked. "My wife said she was going to leave me." "Hasn't she ever said that before?" "Oh yes, hundreds of times. In fact, she has left me twice before. Always came back in a few days." "Well, what was different this time?" The patient replied, "You should have seen the look in her eyes. She wasn't hollering this time."

We instinctively know a genuine crisis. Students of languages say that the word crisis comes from two root words which carry the dual meaning of danger and opportunity. There is a sense that someone is making a move to fundamentally change the nature of things.

A spouse says, "You are sick with your drinking . . . and I am getting sick. So whether you do or not, I'm going to get help. I don't know if our marriage can stand it if I get well and you don't, but I can't let myself be destroyed."

An employer says, "Alice, you've been with this company ten years, and we value your work a lot, but unless you can do something about your drinking we're going to have to let you go.''

A doctor says, ''Ed, you've got some significant liver damage. Let's talk about your drinking. I'm afraid you're going to have to find some way to stop if you want to live.''

One of the significant gains in treating substance dependency in recent years has involved helping families bring such a crisis about at an earlier stage of the illness. It used to be thought that we had to wait for the addicted person to hit bottom—to go through years of deterioration and thereby be motivated by pain to seek help. Now we are seeing that it is possible to raise the bottom so that the sufferer will hit it sooner. Families can, with help from an addiction counselor, design a strategy for intervention with a substance dependent member. The strategy, which must be planned in detail and highly individualized, involves confronting the chemically dependent family member with a united, strong, loving group that may include family, clergyman, doctor, employer and/or very close friend. This group presents the facts without anger. They detail very specifically the suffering they have witnessed in the substance dependent person. They suggest a course of action to begin a program of treatment and recovery. They outline the consequences the dependent person can expect if he or she does not seek help. One counselor calls this ''crisis engineering.'' It has come, in the addiction field, to be called ''intervention.''

# CHAPTER FOUR
## Treatment

Because these illnesses are lived out in family systems, it does not seem to matter a great deal which member of the family comes to this kind of encounter with self first. If any member of the family takes a step toward fundamental change, it raises the possibility that other members may have to consider change. A "good" child is caught stealing at school and asked to see a counselor. A wife develops chronic headaches and is told by the physician that he can either prescribe tranquilizers or recommend a psychiatrist. The psychiatrist is chosen. A husband, who is not usually given to impulsive action, moves out and sues for divorce. A spouse refuses to continue covering up the problem with relatives, friends, and employer (and means it) and seeks help from Al-Anon. A business partner, angry over carrying more than his share of the load, asks out of the partnership—and tells why. These kinds of actions within the systems of relationship tend to unbalance the system in such a way that other members of the system must also consider change.

It will be crucial when such fundamental shifts are taking place, when one or another member of the family system is moving toward help, that the substance dependency be considered as a part of a comprehensive evaluation of the distress. Otherwise there is the risk that a dramatic symptom of the distress, childhood misbehavior at school, for example, or marital distress, might be treated as the only problem.

The longer the substance dependency has been progressing, the more difficult this sorting out may be. What is cause and what is effect becomes confused, and both get lost in a preoccupation with the most troublesome symptom at the time. But treatment and genuine recovery for the whole family must begin in a thorough, comprehensive assessment.

Such assessment for the chemically dependent member will almost always involve some coercion. Perhaps from a spouse, employer, physician, friend, minister, child, or one's own concern for failing health. Often the very first step in treatment and recovery involves understanding the nature of that coercion and coming to terms with the ego wound that it represents. None of us wants to be forced, but the very nature of this illness requires that the force of intruding reality brings one to a readiness, however reluctant or ambivalent, to ask for help.

# When the Chemically Dependent Person Seeks Treatment

When this time comes, one of the most important questions the counselor will ask of the addicted person is, "Why has this come up at this particular time? Why are you here now instead of last month, or instead of waiting until next month?" Exploring the answer to this question in some detail begins to offer both counselor and patient a joint understanding of the particular ambivalence that this unique individual feels in entering treatment.

30

Someone said that ambivalence is what we feel when we see an enemy drive over a cliff in our new car. Webster says it is, "simultaneous attraction toward and repulsion from a person, object, or action." Entering treatment is an action that is always taken in ambivalence. Anyone who has ever waited in a dentist's waiting room knows this. What is sought initially is a way of continuing or modifying the use of chemicals while avoiding the hurtful consequences.

Understanding this, accepting it, exploring it, becomes the basis for the formation of a trusting relationship. It is this relationship with a helper that is at the heart of healing. It is in this relationship of warm mutual regard that the person beginning recovery from addictive illness can begin to explore the experience and feelings about it. It is trusting that the facts and feelings disclosed will be used in this relationship for his benefit that allows the recovering person to penetrate his own denial, learn about the illness, and eventually resolve the ambivalence in favor of a commitment to abstinence.

This ambivalence may turn to clear resistance when the possibility of the family's involvement in the treatment is raised.

— A patient will say,     "No, let's leave her out of it. It's my problem, not hers. Besides she's busy and can't come."

— A spouse says,     "She just has to quit drinking. We don't have any other problems. I really can't do any more."

— A counselor speaks,     "I've always counseled individuals. When relatives get involved, it really becomes difficult to protect the patient from their enabling and offer treatment at the same time."

If we step just behind these words to the feelings, what we

hear is the fear that issues of guilt, blame, and responsibility will be raised too painfully if the spouse or family are involved in treatment. So great is this fear, that it is often twice as difficult to involve family members in treatment as it is to involve substance dependent persons.

Giving these fears a more direct voice, what we hear underlying the specific objections raised above sounds like this: "I sure don't need his coming into treatment with me and telling all over again how bad it's been. I feel bad enough already." "I just can't bear to go into treatment with him and have all this blamed on me again." "If I get her husband into my office with her, I don't know what might happen. How would I handle it? Besides, she's had enough of his abusiveness already. I can help her."

The moralistic, judgmental attitudes our culture holds about these illnesses die hard — even in the counseling office. The counselor here may be seen to be struggling with the same issue the spouse encounters. "What if the situation is more complex than I can handle? How would I feel about myself then?"

Constructive healing relationships are those in which no one has anything to prove. The concepts of fault and blame are not important. Hence, it needs to be understood that family members are involved in treatment not to "spill the beans" about how really bad the substance use has been; not to see what part they play in "causing" the substance dependent person to use his substance (we have seen that causation is much more complex than that). Rather, the family is asked to participate in treatment because all are hurting, all need help.

The opening moves in treatment address the needs of these persons, all members of the family, individually. What is required is a parallel track for recovery of both the substance dependent person and those closest to that person. The basic illness concept of addiction can be learned in a way that sets aside the need of many couples to clarify the question of who is to blame for the substance use. Resolving the intense angers that a couple might bring to the consideration of this question in traditional couples counseling can be a very lengthy and difficult process.

Couples having first had the opportunity to learn about the illness find themselves "ahead of the game" and able to address the core issues, not in terms of blame, but rather in terms of shared grief over illness, shared regrets over behavior, shared sadness over the damage to their relationship. This facilitates acknowledgement of the anger from the past, but also sets a framework for understanding in which the anger can be resolved in forgiveness.

A severe, aging mother of an accomplished professional woman who was suffering drug dependency sat with me in preparation for later sessions with her daughter. She poured out to me the belief that her daughter should simply use her faith, her willpower, and discontinue her bad behavior with chemicals. In almost the same breath she related how hard her own life had been, and how she had had to rely on these inner resources herself without much support from others.

I had already begun working with the daughter and knew that she had incorporated her mother's severity, and, in addition to her drug dependency, suffered from a severe conscience. This kept her so driven in her quest for excellence that often the only relief she knew was that brief time between the onset of substance use and the loss of control. This woman felt that despite years of attempting to measure up to her mother's expectations, and, despite considerable achievement in her profession, she had never received her mother's blessing. Thus, the continuation of mother's severe attitudes towards her only enabled her dependency to proceed, raised her guilty anxiety to intolerable proportions, and gave her a rationale for continued use.

As I confronted the mother with the illness concept of

addiction and with my own experience and that of other patients; that faith and willpower alone do not always deliver us from our human bondage, she began to share her own sense of limits and her severity towards herself.

This laid the groundwork for the next session to which the daughter was invited. The mother could never have advanced so quickly in her daughter's presence. Their struggle for blessing had been going for too long and was too rigid to allow her to express this much in her presence.

Now together, both having some understanding of the illness of addiction and their participation in it, when her daughter told this mother of her life-long struggle for her blessing, the mother surprised her utterly by confessing her need for her daughter's blessing. It was one of those beautiful moments in counseling when people seem to grow by new creation rather than by the more common hard work. Mother confessed that much of her pushing her daughter to excell academically and professionally had its genesis in her painful sense of her own limited education. The hour ended with a measure of healing which enabled them both to begin giving to each other those blessings which are real and saying no to those demands which are not.

This illustration makes clear the benefit of some separateness at the earliest stage of treatment. One effect of these illnesses is to drive family members abnormally close to each other. There is a loss of individuality, and a single unit of pain and struggle is created in which each tries to draw closer to the other so as to help the family regain control. This creates a loss of perspective, individuality and love.

Given a structure of treatment that temporarily addresses individual needs then turns to family needs, there is the opportunity to regain a strong sense of personal goals, allow time for the addicted person to detoxify, and gain an understanding of the illness that the whole family can share as it begins the work of repairing the family as a unit.

# The Parallel Track of Early Recovery

Treatment begins in understanding. There is a need for a thorough *assessment* of the substance dependent person, spouse and children — at the very least, that one person who is closest and, therefore, most involved in the illness.

This thorough assessment for the dependent person will involve a comprehensive drug history. The important thing here is not filling in the blanks with information to be stored in a chart and forgotten. The interpersonal process involved in the patient giving and the counselor receiving this data is one in which trust begins to be built. This working pair of counselor and patient begins to evolve a joint understanding of how and when pleasurable use evolved into abusive overuse, and how that evolved into addiction. This understanding begins to relieve the patient of some of the fear and isolation. Here is someone who understands. And looking back with that someone, the patient begins to understand. As one patient said to me after having reviewed this history with her counselor, "Boy, I thought he was going to ask me if I beat my kids when I get drunk, which I don't, but he began by asking if I remembered the first drink I ever had in my life."

Alongside this alcohol and drug history, the dependent person will also detail a life history. This is a narrative account of one's life that particularly highlights certain areas: childhood, memories of parents and their relationship, school, adolescence and the beginning of dating, how one came to leave home, education, employment, military service, sexual functioning, children, a review of problems in any area of life, particular life experiences that contributed to maturing or slowing some aspects of development, social, cultural, and religious identity, important illnesses and previous treatment, hopes and plans, those areas of personal or relational growth that have been slowed or halted by the addictive illness, the particular sources of growth, pleasure, and recreation that have been important and what has happened to these under the impact of the illness.

*The Spouse* or other family member needs a similar assessment. This is an assessment of interaction patterns — the response he or she has evolved living in close emotional proximity to one suffering addictive illness. What feelings has this person felt? What strategies for coping have been tried — with what effect upon the emotional life and physical energy? In what ways has the family restructured itself in order to attempt to deal with the chronic sense of crisis? What is likely to happen to these patterns of restructuring if they are rendered unnecessary by recovery? What is the remaining level of commitment to the marriage? How are the children feeling, thinking, and behaving? What do the family members expect from treatment — for themselves and their addicted relative? What will these persons do if the addict recovers? If he or she does not? How do they understand the substance dependency — what need is there for education about it? What level of awareness do they have of their own participation and need for help as opposed to a fearful or angry, "He just needs to stop. Then everything else will be fine."

These assessments lead to a working diagnosis and treatment plan. After several days of inpatient care, or a few appointments on an outpatient basis, patient and family should be able to expect an open sharing of the professional assessment — the diagnosis and an estimate of its severity. This should encompass the primary patient and the family.

*Withdrawal* is one of the primary goals of early treatment. This represents the time of maximum physical discomfort and danger to the addicted person. It represents, for the family, a time of mixed relief that something is being done and often fearful wondering if it will be adequate — that is, a time of refocusing on their own anxieties.

Withdrawal from addictive substances is often an acute

medical emergency. It can threaten life. The symptoms, severity, and the course the withdrawal will take, depend upon the specific substances the patient has used, in what combinations, and in what amounts, over what length of time, and the patient's general state of physical health. Symptoms may include: nervousness, anxiety, irritability, sweating, elevated blood pressure and pulse rate, sleep disturbance, depression, appetite and digestive disturbance, fear, agitation, hypersensitivity to sound, light, and touch, shakiness, hallucinations, disorientation, and seizures. The more severe and life-threatening manifestations can generally be prevented or controlled by good medical care. The pattern is to use medications which control these symptoms and reduce the dose as quickly as possible. The medications used frequently have addicting potential themselves, but careful control of dose and length of use prevents complicating the problem by cross-addiction. Physicians who have a thorough understanding of addiction, and their number is growing, do not prescribe these drugs (notably the minor tranquilizers, Valium, Librium, Atavan) for anxiety management in addicted persons beyond the period of time required for detoxification.

Typically, with the drug alcohol, the acute and most distressing symptoms of withdrawal pass within a matter of a few days with good care. More minor symptoms, such as sleep disturbance may continue for several weeks. Some observers report periodic return of symptoms, though in lessening severity, over the first year of sobriety. This phenomenon has also been observed with Valium addiction.

Until withdrawal has been completely accomplished, and the individual has had several days drug-free, the risk of relapse and return to addictive use is extremely high if treatment is interrupted. The process of withdrawal is frequently so uncomfortable that until it is completed, the patient has only two alternatives: completion of medically supervised withdrawal, or a return to self-medication of the symptoms with the addicting substance.

Many persons do not realize they are addicted until they attempt to discontinue the chemical use. This is a time of feeling worse before they can feel better. The experience of withdrawal is, for many patients, a powerful confrontation with the reality of their disease.

A good physical examination at this stage of treatment is well-advised. General health problems may have been neglected because of preoccupation with the addiction. The damage done to body systems by the abusive use also needs to be assessed and reported to the patient.

The family is beginning its recovery at this time also. If the addicted patient has been hospitalized, he or she may feel a sense of relief. This may quickly pass, and visits or telephone calls may produce a request by the primary patient for support in terminating inpatient care. The patient experiences physical discomfort and anxiety-producing confrontation with the reality of the nature and extent of their problem. The family will need resources of support to toughen their love. It is sometimes more loving to say no than to say yes.

Conversations in the family during these days may be characterized by more than the usual amount of tension. For the family member, who has held out the hope that if the addicted family member would simply discontinue chemical use things would be much better, it may come as quite a shock that things may get worse for awhile. Persons in withdrawal are frequently edgy, irritable, and anger is close to the surface. I have heard family members say during this time, "We were better off when he was drinking." It is fortunate that this period usually passes rather quickly.

Following detoxification there comes, for patient and family, the discipline of living one day at a time with the new situation. Subjective experience of these first days varies greatly. One patient looking back on a long term recovery of years' duration remembered her first month as, "thirty days and three hundred nights." Others experience an elation and rising hope that leads them to prematurely conclude, "This isn't going to be as big a deal as I thought. I'm OK now and just need to get back in the swing of things." Similarly, family members may find themselves swinging between rising hopes and anxiously wondering how long it will last.

The patient is now withdrawn from the drug. The family has some grounds for hope. But the new resources that will support continuing recovery are not yet in place. Stability has been achieved, but stability will have to become growth if genuine lasting recovery is to be sustained. The situation is somewhat like that depicted by the story of the house where the devil has been cast out, but precisely because of the emptiness of the house, seven devils occupy it. One of the toughest challenges in recovering from addiction is created by the fact that abstinence must be established before the growth that can sustain it can flourish. Hence, the supportive advice of A.A. and Al-Anon, "One day at a time."

The major task of early recovery for patient and family is to come to an understanding of the nature of addictive illness and acceptance of its personal reality. The addicted person needs help to overcome the denial of the illness on an intellectual and emotional level. The illusion of control over the substance needs to fall away. "We admitted that we were powerless over alcohol — that our lives had become unmanageable."* It is with the simplicity of genius that A.A. has placed this step at the beginning of its description of the process of recovery from addiction. Without that step, there is no place to begin; indeed there is no perceived need for the journey.

It is the same for the close family member. Just as the

---

*Step One of the Twelve Steps of Alcoholics Anonymous from *Alcoholics Anonymous*, (New York: A.A. General Services Inc., 1976), p. 59.

addicted member must admit powerlessness, so must the family members. The lack of an understanding of the illness leads to the delusion of control. "We had an argument, and she took too many of those pills again last night. After I picked her up and got her in bed, I decided to just throw them out." This, again, is a way of not seeing the reality that I am powerless to control her decision to take pills.

Recovery for all begins in a parallel giving up of the fantasy of control. This involves giving up some of our wish for omnipotence and surrendering to reality. "Once I begin using mood-changing substances I lose my freedom of choice." And for the spouse, "There is nothing I can do to make her use those substances or make her stop. That's not in my power."

The denial has begun to crack. When it does, there is a transitory period of discouragement. The enormity of the illness and the task of recovery comes home for the dependent person. "What will I be like without my pills?" "How can I possibly face my old drinking buddies?" "What will I do with all that time?" "Will my spouse still love me?"

With good treatment, a corner is turned where primary patient and family encounter a paradox. The acceptance of powerlessness over the substance brings one to a new sense of mastery and hopefulness. As a patient in a therapy group said to a newcomer, "It's strange, but when I began to see that I had lost control . . . when I began to see the illness, once I got over the shock, I felt more in charge. Seeing it now I can be responsible for it."

How different a thing this kind of responsibility for an illness is from the guilt that is experienced when substance dependency is seen as a failing over which one should exercise more control. When one comes to understand addiction as an illness — not chosen, not something consciously allowed to happen, the energy that used to be used to defend against public censure and private awareness becomes available for growth.

The hope for all of us is that as we come to understand the process of illness and health, the more we have the ability to respond (literally to be response-able) with an appropriate self-regard for the wonder of creation.

For the addicted person and family this means a deep down, emotionally-based commitment to continued learning and growth. It means for the spouse a renewed commitment to self. It means that for at least the next year and perhaps for a lifetime, there will be a need for readily available support from persons who understand the illness — a conscious cultivation of the alternatives to bondage.

# CHAPTER FIVE
## Recovery

Alcohol and drug dependency command attention. Everyone notices. The further it progresses, the more attention it receives. This requires a great deal of energy and abnormally concentrates the focus of the family on an area that normally claims only a small part of our attention. Our capacity to attend to and respond to a given number of things in the course of a day is, of course, limited. The practical implication of all of this is that by a too exclusive attention to the drug dependency other things are overlooked. Even important things have to be delayed, forgotten, put on hold because of the fixation on the chemical use.

If recovery is to proceed, this process must now be powerfully reversed. The focus must be broadened. Areas of relationship too long neglected must be brought up-to-date and examined. Old pleasures must be reclaimed. Battles postponed must now be looked at. Love unexpressed and buried under resentment must now be resurrected. It is as though with a mind now clear of the chemical influence and the reality of the illness accepted, the family now turns to the task of rebuilding. As one man said about a month into recovery when he was enjoying some of the results of the hard work done thus far, "This is great, but it's not enough. There has got to be more to life than staying sober."

The focus now broadens from being an addicted person, and the struggle to integrate all that this means, to being a *recovering* addicted person. Put another way, the focus moves from illness to health for all members of the family.

A woman learned from her doctor that she was diabetic. Her response included denial, anger at the injustice, grief for the lost pleasure of sugar, much strategizing to meet the necessary changes in diet, learning how to live with the experience of being "different" at a social dinner, learning how to tell others so as to establish the ground rules for the shared pleasure of eating without feeling the necessity of going into a complete medical history or eliciting pity. All of this took weeks, months.

Finally there came a time when, having done all of this necessary early work, she came to a new understanding. She described it in a letter to her son: "When I first learned of the diagnosis, all I was for a while was diabetic. I could think of nothing else. It seemed such a total, terrible inconvenience. Such an abrupt intrusion into my life. Now that I'm beginning to get some handles on managing it, I realize that I'm not just a diabetic. I'm also a mother, a wife, a friend, a church attender, a neighbor, a person who loves to sew and watch scarey movies, really a person who, except for being diabetic, is in pretty good shape."

Something like that must happen in recovery from another chronic illness — addiction. Personal growth; reclaiming old tricks and learning new ones, experiencing old pleasures that used to include substance use *without* the substance, learning new ways of relieving stress, breaking the bonds of rigid ways of behaving, and learning how to adjust behavior to the real demands of the immediate situation — all of this represents the full flowering of recovery.

The addicted member and the family need to clarify the specifics of these goals for themselves and begin to practice some new behaviors. All of us are somewhat limited in our bag of tricks for coping with the many varied situations that life daily presents to us. Because of the accident of who we grew up around, and their preferred style of coming to terms with life, all of us have coping mechanisms that come naturally and others we are hardly familiar with. The more coping mechanisms we have, the less likely we are to experience an overload of stress. Hence, increasing one's options is a wise move, not only in supporting sobriety, but in making sobriety more enjoyable for the entire family.

The following self-test has been used with a great many people and is helpful for family members to clarify those areas where one may feel experienced and those areas where one may feel the need to learn.

**"Increasing One's Options"**          Name:_____
                                         Date:_____

Living in this world is a very complex business. In the course of an average day, we will encounter a variety of people in a variety of situations. And we will be expected to behave somewhat differently in these different situations. There are times when it will be best to stand up for ourselves and times when it will be best to give in; times when it will be best to plan what to do and times when it will be best not to plan; times when it will be best to be playful and times when it will be best to be serious; etc., etc. Hopefully, we have all learned many of these different ways of relating and have gotten a lot of practice at them. But we are all limited to some extent. And if we have only learned a very few ways of relating to our world, then our lives will feel very cramped and limited. If we have never had any practice in standing up for ourselves, for instance, if we only know how to give in to people, then there are many situations that we will handle very poorly, and we will end up feeling terrible.

The purpose of this listing is to get some practice in relatively new ways of relating. Please go through this list and check the things you would like to practice more and those you feel you do well.

---------------

| I need more practice at this | I feel I do this well | |
|---|---|---|
| _____ | _____ | Cooperating with other people. |
| _____ | _____ | Asking people to cooperate with me. |
| _____ | _____ | Asking people for help. |
| _____ | _____ | Standing up for myself. |
| _____ | _____ | Compromising, giving in to other people. |
| _____ | _____ | Asking people to do favors for me. |
| _____ | _____ | Doing favors for people, offering help to people. |
| _____ | _____ | Learning to say no . . . not being taken advantage of. |
| _____ | _____ | Accepting compliments and other expressions of affection. |
| _____ | _____ | Complimenting other people. |
| _____ | _____ | Handling criticism. |
| _____ | _____ | Offering helpful ideas to other people. |
| _____ | _____ | Refusing to accept insults. |
| _____ | _____ | Taking the first step in meeting people. |

| I need more practice at this | I feel I do this well | |
|---|---|---|
| ———— | ———— | Letting other people know how I really feel. |
| ———— | ———— | Making decisions on my own, and sticking with them. |
| ———— | ———— | Being able to change my mind. |
| ———— | ———— | Being assertive, making sure I don't get left out of things. |
| ———— | ———— | Making sure my life isn't boring. |
| ———— | ———— | Having fun. |
| ———— | ———— | Listening. |
| ———— | ———— | Saying what I want to say. |
| ———— | ———— | Knowing how and when to laugh. |
| ———— | ———— | Being able to weep. |
| ———— | ———— | Being able to follow through with what I start or what I promise. |
| ———— | ———— | Carrying my share of the load. |
| ———— | ———— | Sticking with a job — or school — housework — etc., even if it's unpleasant. |
| ———— | ———— | Acting civilized in public — being willing to follow rules that seem stupid to me. |
| ———— | ———— | Learning how to trust people. |
| ———— | ———— | Learning how to decide who not to trust. |
| ———— | ———— | Knowing when, where and how to express angry feelings. |
| ———— | ———— | Controlling my temper. |
| ———— | ———— | Being able to express loving feelings. |
| ———— | ———— | Finding ways to express loving feelings. |
| ———— | ———— | Being pleased with my successes. |
| ———— | ———— | Being able to live with my imperfections. |

| I need more practice at this | I feel I do this well | |
|---|---|---|
| _____ | _____ | To stop torturing myself for my mistakes and forgive myself. |
| _____ | _____ | Forgiving other people. |
| _____ | _____ | (List some other areas that pertain to you.) |
| _____ | _____ | |
| _____ | _____ | |
| _____ | _____ | *Please circle the three areas above where you feel you need the most help. |

This instrument becomes a contract with the family for change; an agreement to work together to establish some new ground; a commitment to trying on some new behavior to see how it feels. The counseling relationship becomes a safe place where new behavior may be tried, then discussed, without fear of ridicule. It will be expected that new steps will be awkward and often filled with anxiety. But this is the kind of awkwardness and anxiety that, experienced to the depths, begins to free us to grow.

## Reversal of Isolation

One cannot recover from addictive illness alone. The course of the disease isolates the sufferers. This isolation must be dealt with if recovery is to continue. Shame over drug-induced behavior vanishes amid an accepting group that understands the illness. The shame, which is an anxiety that can only lead to renewed substance use for the dependent person, is changed into self-understanding and is socialized into identification with the community of recovering persons.

The first step of A.A. begins "*We . . .*" There is power in a community with shared understandings, shared commitments, shared hopes.

The spouse now needs to continue to give attention to ways to break an unhealthy absorption in the life of the addicted partner. A new member of an open counseling group for spouses of alcoholics introduced herself to the group by telling them how bad her husband's alcoholism had been, all the various strategies she had tried to control it, how none of them had worked. She concluded with the statement, "I'm just on the verge of giving up!" This was said in a way that conveyed that, in her view, giving up was the worst possible thing she could do. How totally surprised she was when an older member of the group replied, "Great! Wouldn't that be a marvelous relief!"

The more experienced older member went on to share all that he was doing to make sure that he maintained this posture of surrender and continued to focus his energies on reversing the isolation in which he had become trapped. As he continued to "give up" on controlling his spouse's alcoholism it became important to reclaim a life of his own; new friends, old associations and interests, refusing to have his life controlled by the sobriety or intoxication of his partner.

## Help for the Marriage

A woman looks at her husband across a dinner table, after a meal eaten in silence, and speaks what they are both thinking. "Do we really have a marriage now that we no longer have your problem? There's been so little else between us for so long."

Chemical dependency is a chronic progressive disease that has usually been present for some time before it is treated. One result of this is that once the addiction is treated, and some sobriety established, there may still be severe problems in the marriage that require professional help.

A recovering woman alcoholic says to her counselor: "Now that I've been sober four months, I'm suddenly aware that our marriage died a long time ago. My problem got all the attention; but now I see he's so full of problems of his own that I just don't even like him any more."

How different these concerns are from the trap both these couples were caught in when they first entered treatment. One of the couples had been to a marriage counselor in the hope that if they just got their relationship straightened out, the "drinking problem" would disappear. They had both really tried to be open to the counseling process, but the addiction rolled progressively onward like the disease that it is.

The other couple had at first come to treatment full of blaming. "If you would just get off my back, I could handle the drinking." "The only thing that's wrong in our family is your drinking. If you would just stop, everything would be all right."

Now, several months later after proper treatment that paid attention first to the addictive illness, both these couples were able to see that the destructive drinking was the primary problem, but also that because it was so primary, other problems in the relationship had been overlooked. Now, having come to understand the addiction, these people were ready to look at the whole of their relationship and think through with someone what they wanted to do about the damage.

The marriage partners need time in which to look carefully at their responses to the disease, what that response has cost them, and to begin to get some separateness and a sense of their own lives again. The negotiating for the healing of the marriage that will come later needs to be a discussion between two separate and equal selves. Often in the response to the alcoholism, the non-addicted partner has lost that sense of being a separate self who has a sense of worth.

In the fashion typical of family response in any chronic progressive disease, the marriage partner has often become almost totally absorbed. Quite often, the whole of life seems caught up in efforts to control the uncontrollable; in grief for the lost love; in self-blame. Treatment then begins in exploring together *the changes in the relationship as both adapted to the addictive disease* — and what this has cost.

The adaptation to the primary addictive illness is usually the source of most of the difficulty in the marriage. Both have adapted to the disease, and while this is not the cause of the drinking, it is vitally important in understanding why the marriage is threatened.

Some themes come up so often as couples work together to repair the damage, that they are worth consideration by almost all couples going through this process.

1.  *One is regression. Regression means going backward. In human terms, going backward in our development; becoming silly, dependent, childish. It can be fun, and we are seeking the pleasure of regression when we play. But what makes it fun is the time-limited quality of it and our knowledge that we can come back to our adult state if and when we need to.*

But for the addict, and his partner, regression is a horrifying trip down a greased slide with the fear that they may never be able to climb up again. They progressively lose the capacity for normal adult social functioning and pull back in guilt and isolation like a child who has been punished and ostracized from the disapproving society. Regression means withdrawal. Regression may be seen when a chemically dependent person:

> becomes less able to share the leadership of a family.

> asks the marriage partner to conduct the family relationships with those outside — phone calls, appointments, excuses for absence from work.

turns over management of the finances to the spouse.

is no longer able to be consistent as a parent and delegates most discipline of children to the other parent.

Regression may be seen when the marriage partner:

begins dropping out of social relationships in order to take care of the alcoholic.

feels responsible for everything that happens, yet helpless.

gets so distracted as to be unable to function effectively.

gets sick.

The hallmark of regression is *dependency*. To go backward in our development is to return to a dependent state. If you have to be hospitalized for appendicitis this afternoon and spend several days in the hospital, you are going to regress. You will become dependent on others to relieve your pain, provide you with drugs, bring your meals. And, once the worst pain is over you are probably not going to like being that dependent on others — you may even get angry at them.

This is precisely what happens between the addict and spouse. As the addictive disease progresses, the substance dependent member regresses . . . becomes more dependent . . . the spouse responds by becoming the caretaker . . . both resent the dependency relationship . . . and anger follows.

Before treatment, however, there has been no helpful way of talking about anger. Attempts to do so become occasions for more nonproductive blaming. Sitting down with someone who they feel to be wise about life, marriage partners may now begin to talk about the changes of responsibility and roles they have lived through. The spouse may say angrily,

"He says he wants the checkbook back. How can I let go when, for all I know tomorrow he may blow it all on a drunk." The dependent person says with no less anger, "That's the way it always is . . . she won't let go!"

Help can come as these people begin to realize, and share with each other, the whole range of feelings they have had about this problem of roles in the family. The counselor will probably respond, "It's evident that you both have a lot of anger about this. I wonder what other feelings you remember as you look back on how you got into this situation, where you, John, no longer have access to the checkbook."

And the addicted person begins to remember and share the sadness and despair he felt when the addiction began to rob him of his manly strength. And the spouse gets in touch with her fear of always having to be strong. And more than they have in years, this couple begins to exchange a broad range of feelings that gives them common ground to face what they are up against together, and renegotiate the roles and power alignments. It seems important that now sober and beginning to communicate, each say to the other what they will and will not be responsible for.

As this illustration makes clear, what is needed as partners begin to repair their marriage is a way of getting back in touch. The couple needs to begin to *share a broader range of feelings* — not just the blaming and anger (though ventilating that while sober may be an important first step). As they can share also the regret, the guilt, the fears, the sadness, the frustrated hopes — there may be created, or re-created, a lively core of a solid relationship.

2. *Another common concern is stagnation. Some describe it as "fixation." Others describe the "learning deficit" that grows as a result of the stagnation. Whatever we call it, couples seem to experience it as a felt need to "catch up."*

A young couple has been married three years, but she has been suffering an addictive illness for seven years. Suddenly, after a period of treatment, she wakes up really straight for the first time in her marriage. And both begin to feel what it's like to be together in a way they never have before. And so they begin to talk with a counselor, and more importantly, with each other. And in a hundred ways, they begin to be aware that they have missed out on some of the learning that couples ordinarily go through in the first couple of years of marriage. The learning deficit becomes obvious as they ask:

"How do we ever begin to talk to each other now that we no longer have your problem to talk about?"

"How can we learn to disagree and fight fair without fear of violence or retreat into depressed silence?"

"What are you really like, this person I've lived with three years?"

"How can we learn to help each other out in periods of normal mood changes and anxiety?"

It is as though they have stood still, stagnant, since their wedding day.

Or, another clinical illustration of the fixation in the family: a wife in a spouses group says, "Yes, he's been sober two months, but he's driving me crazy . . . he treats the children like they are little kids . . . they're teenagers!"

A good history taking quickly told us what was going on. This man had become addicted after ten years of good parenting of his kids, but he had been addicted for the last six years. In those years of addictive illness, there had developed a learning deficit as a consequence of addiction. Because the addiction had rendered him *emotionally unavailable*, he had not had the opportunity to learn gradually, over a period of years, the difference between parenting a small child and parenting an adolescent.

But for this couple, coming to understand it this way gave them a new perspective on the problem, a new insight into what they were up against together with their children, and, in some ways, a new relationship in which to offer parenting as a couple.

What the learning deficit points to is the fact that over the typical several years between the development of addiction and the onset of treatment, couples are not able to sustain that pleasure/tension balance that produces growth and learning. Coming to see ordinary manifestations of this, to identify it as a consequence of the addictive illness and beginning to pick up the work that has been postponed are important elements in recovery of the marriage.

"Picking up the work that has been postponed" — that is not a bad description of what couples suffering from addiction must do once sobriety is established and the addiction treated. Frequently, this comes as a surprise. When you have survived the worst, there is an understandable desire for a period of "peace and quiet." But, as one couple who had tried this approach (tried settling for sobriety and not paying attention to the deterioration of their relationship) said when re-entering treatment, "There's got to be more to life than just staying sober." Indeed there has.

Indeed, there has got to be more. There is more to life than the struggle not to drink — and that more is the affirmation of what one most deeply wants to do. There is more than a constant effort to regain control of one's life — and that more is the release and enjoyment of letting go. There is more than sobriety (the last meaning my dictionary gives that word is, "sedateness: gravity") — and that more is joy. There is more than the self-sufficiency of those who have survived the worst — and that more is intimacy.

## The Children

If it has not come up already, certainly the needs of children in a recovering family will come to the fore during treatment. Children will almost certainly need help understanding and accepting the changes the family will move through on the way to health.

Most likely, children have learned, during the most chaotic phases of the addictive illness, to relate to both parents in adaptive ways that will now need to change. A twelve-year-old said, during a counseling session with her parents, "Mom and I had just learned not to listen to Dad because he didn't mean what he said a lot of the time — or he would forget it later. It sure is different now. He gets mad when we don't listen. I'm not sure which way I like him better." Here is a child struggling to come to terms with change. Even when it is for the better, change threatens adaptations that have been constructed for good reason. Therefore, fear and resistance are involved. This child will need opportunities to discuss with her father her mixed feelings about the changes she experiences as he reclaims his authority. She will need the supportive counsel of mother — and mother's example — as father begins to be taken seriously again.

Many children in this position are having to give up something — which is to say that they struggle with loss as a parent recovers. They have usually learned over time to use the guilt of the substance abusing parent. As one adolescent son said, "I knew I could get anything out of Mom when she was sobering up." These children will struggle with the fantasy that the parent's return to drinking would be better. Often the reassertion of parental authority will have to be discussed with the child. The recovering parent will need to indicate understanding of the child's mixed feelings, allow the child to ventilate past angers, but also to make clear that he or she is back on the scene, and the child is going to have to deal with them.

The healing of the marriage itself is the key to the adaptation of the children to the recovery. Children will be slower to adapt when they sense that their parents have not truly done the work to repair their own relationship. Each of our children may be envisioned as having three parents; a mother, a father, and the relationship between mother and father. That relationship *parents* them. The relationship between parents presents for children the possibilities for resolving conflict; it instructs them in the expression of affection. Similarly, that relationship suggests to the child either that he must come to terms with its solidity, or that he may be successful in using the crack in the relationship for his own manipulative advantage.

## Relapse

A return to the use of mood-changing substances represents a relapse. The Merriam-Webster Dictionary says that relapse means: "to slip back into a former condition (as of illness) after a change for the better."

Like all chronic diseases, addiction is characterized by relapse. This does not mean that everyone who begins recovery will at some time return to a period of use. It does mean that when this does happen, we will not be totally surprised. The substance dependent person, and the family, will be hurt, remorseful, discouraged, angry. But if they have understood the nature of the illness, they will not be unprepared for the possibility.

In this event several things will need to be addressed:

1. The reassertion of denial and rationalization that made relapse possible will need to be discussed, identified, and understood.

2. The angry feelings at one's self following relapse will need

to be resolved. These angry feelings at self may be expressed as regret, depression, guilt, remorse, shame, or projected as anger at someone else.

3. Self-acceptance will need to evolve out of a deeper understanding of the illness and the goal for recovery. Total abstinence for a lifetime is the last goal on the road of recovery. For many persons an intermediate goal must be longer periods of abstinence and shorter periods of relapse. The person who comes into treatment following years of addiction, then experiences four months of abstinence, followed by a five-day relapse, followed by early return to treatment and beginning to be abstinent again has made a good deal of progress. This is not to say that relapses are to be taken lightly. Particularly if the pattern becomes one of shorter periods of abstinence or longer periods of relapse (rather than quick return to treatment), the recovering person will need to confront, and be confronted by, this pattern.

4. The need of the family members, particularly the one person closest to the addict, to continue during the relapse to take care of themselves rather than being drawn into their own relapse by focusing all their attention in attempts to manage the addict. Taking care of self may involve finding someone to share the feelings of disappointment and anger with. It may involve taking direct steps to protect one's self from drug-affected behavior. It may involve a planned separation. Many families at this time will need help sorting out what they can and cannot do for the addicted person.

5. As an addicted person may undermine his or her own sobriety by unconsciously engaging in denial and rationalization, it is also possible that family members have unconsciously undermined the recovery process because

of their discomfort with what the new situation represents. This possibility will need to at least be considered and evaluated. An example may be seen in the wife of an alcoholic who confided, "You know, while God knows I was glad for his recovery, there was another level at which it scared me. Now the focus was back on me and my problems. I wasn't ready for that."

## Spiritual Recovery

Whether one conceives of it in traditional terms or not, recovery from addiction has a spiritual dimension for the addicted person and for the family members. Totally fulfilling recovery represents a healing of body, mind, and spirit. These facets of human nature cannot be separated. Whatever heals our body also influences how we think about things and lifts our spirits. Whatever heals the spirit, making us more hopeful, also positively influences our ability to think straight and feel good physically.

At some point in recovery, attention will turn to these matters. When that time comes, several themes typically come forward.

Addiction makes us painfully aware of the choices we all make between life and death. Choosing life requires us to explore, in very individual ways, the well-springs of creativity within us. It also requires us to look deeply and become more self-aware of the capacity for self-destruction that is in all of us. Choosing life is a spiritual process.

Addiction faces us with the spiritual task of finding the courage to face our anxieties, rather than anesthetizing them. Finding a source of courage is one of the basic spiritual tasks of adulthood. The willingness to engage in the search without demanding that all our fears be set aside first is perhaps the beginning place, the journey, and the destination all at once.

Addiction causes us to behave in ways that conflict with our personal value systems. This produces guilt and shame.

Recovery will involve reclaiming, reconstructing, and hopefully growing in that value system. Suffering can make us bitter, harsh, judgmental people. It can also make us more understanding of human failings — our own and those of others. Spiritual recovery often calls on us to integrate the themes of forgiveness and judgment found in the great religions.

Addiction forces us to admit that we are not God. It bruises our omnipotence. There are some things I cannot beat. There are some battles I cannot win. I am not self-sufficient. I need the community . . . the recovering community . . . the worshipping community . . . the community of man.

What spiritual recovery nudges us toward is the discovery that we are human — and that this is enough. Spiritual maturity draws us to the conclusion that in human life there is no absolute certainty, no absolute knowing, no absolute safety from anxiety. Spiritual maturity affirms that these things are not needed for life to be blessed. It is enough that we trust, that we hope, that we have faith.

# AFTERWORD
## Getting Help

If you are concerned about the drinking or medication use of some family members, there are two steps you can take: seek the help of A.A. or Al-Anon (phone numbers are listed in most directories), and go for a professional evaluation. If the person who appears to have a problem with substances will not go — go alone.

Al-Anon is a self-help support group for persons who are emotionally close to those suffering alcohol dependency. It offers a way of understanding the illness, a way of understanding the traps that those who live close to it can fall into, and a way out of those traps. Alateen does the same for teenagers. Most towns have several groups. Choosing one may be like choosing a church, or a friend, or a club. You may not like the first group you will visit. You may want to go several times and then try another group until you feel that you are with people who can help you.

Many otherwise competent professionals are not experienced

in treating problems of substance use, abuse and addiction. One of the following resources should be able to help you find one who is: your minister, priest or rabbi, your family doctor, your area mental health center, your state department of mental health, an area alcohol and drug council, an A.A. or Al-Anon member.

You should be able to expect the following kinds of assistance from the counselor or agency:

a.  a caring rather than judgmental attitude on the part of your professional helper;

b.  a careful evaluation of the history of alcohol and drug use — physical, emotional, and social consequences. This should lead your helper to be able to share frankly with you his estimate of the nature of the problem — the stage of the substance problem, and the prospect for treatment, if any is recommended;

c.  medical care for the withdrawal syndrome (physical distress when the substance is discontinued);

d.  recognition of and response to both the needs of the chemically dependent person and other family members — a treatment plan that includes both;

e.  an opportunity to learn, in considerable detail, the nature of addictive illness and problems associated with its management; and

f.  opportunity to participate in designing a plan of treatment specifically tailored to the needs of your family.

If your first attempts to locate professional help lead you to someone not prepared to offer all of these things, move on. Seeing a professional person for an evaluation does not bind you to continue treatment with him or her. Keep looking until you find someone you feel comfortable with. Stay long enough (at least several months) to get what you need.

An expert consulting teacher was teaching a class for qualified teachers. Through each of his lectures he wrote key points on the blackboard. Each lecture was ended when he wrote on the board: "TINEW." The curiosity of the class, teachers who had come to learn new techniques and sharpen their skills, grew with each session. It was not until the final class, at the end of two weeks, that the professor revealed the meaning. He wrote on the board:

```
TINEW    T  I  N  E  W
         H  S  O  A  A
         E     S  Y
         R     Y
         E
```

Quick fix-it-up formulas will not avail. The fact that there is no easy way leads us at times to conclude that there is no way — but there is. Only faith at first, and then experience, can teach us that the struggles to grow are worth it.

# About the Author

James E. Burgin grew up in a family touched by alcoholism and in a church with strong anti-alcohol convictions. All of this found a new synthesis, nurtured in change, when he entered the addiction field professionally.

He entered the ministry of the Church of God (Anderson, Indiana) after taking his masters degree in theology. His counseling experience as a parish pastor led him to seek two years of clinical pastoral education. Following this he was certified by the National Association for Clinical Pastoral Education as a training supervisor of clergy in clinical training.

In 1970, he became chaplain supervisor at the Georgia Clinic in Atlanta, Georgia. Subsequently he served as unit director of the addiction rehabilitation unit of the Georgia Mental Health Institute in Atlanta and as clinical director of the alcoholism program of Clayton Mental Health Center.

In 1980, Chaplain Burgin became program director at Fenwick Hall, a private chemical dependency treatment center in Charleston, South Carolina.

Previous publications include, "Help for the Marriage Partner of an Alcoholic," published by Hazelden in 1976. He has been a speaker for five years at the annual meeting of the Alcohol and Drug Problems Association of North America.